Mehmet

AF623618

Alison Diaz

BookLeaf Publishing

Presentation by *BookLeaf Publishing*

Web: www.bookleafpub.com

E-mail: info@bookleafpub.com

ISBN: 9789357212120

First edition 2023

DEDICATION

My indelible friend, here are the love letters I could not send. You have touched me in permanent ways.

ACKNOWLEDGEMENT

Thank you to my loved ones for always
believing there is value to my craft.

PREFACE

They say that when an artist falls in love with you, you will never die.

Here my sweet and deliciously deadly Mehmet, I attempt to immortalize you inside my humble cage of cloying words.

You've Got Mail

The same way I introduced myself as your friend, I say goodbye.

Curious eyes, calling me to engage.

I wrote you letters, before I even knew what they were.

Hello I said, I like to write.

You said you liked to read them.

So I continued.

Rebel

I have daddy issues, I told you early on.

Attracted to the unavailable.

Chasing who does not want me.

I played myself.

How could I know I would end up craving
tracing the shape of your knee with my
fingertips.

What Do You Like

You made me feel seen.

You made me feel wanted. You made me feel smart.

Always asking for my opinion and taking my advice.

Did you know I would fall in love with you.

Was my need for your approval so obvious.

10:00 pm, 14/09/20

Mehmet,

I am dying to hear your voice. I just want to text you asking you for a voice note, but I don't want to be needy. I miss you so much. You have no idea.

I Didn't Get The Job, 12/11/20

Mehmet,

There is nothing more romantic to me than you offering to break someone's legs with a baseball bat for me.

How could I now love you?

ps. Why am I so tragically turned on my violence?

Early On

You told me a secret.

One I will never repeat, not even here.

I think you expected my recoil, instead of my sympathy.

I will always treasure your moments of trust and vulnerability with me.

I will always love you and keep your secrets.

26/11/20

Mehmet,

Baby, it's almost time for me to go now. I love you. I'm not leaving you. I never will. Just like I'll never send this letter.

Today I got notice that it's probable I'll be leaving before the end of the year. It's going to be so hard to say goodbye. I treasure every second with you. I'm going to miss you dearly.

28/12/20

I will keep this food in my belly tonight and not think about how I don't have you.

Gemini Season 04/06/2020

Shroom Trip.

I know what love is baby.
This is Love. You are love.
Forever, my love.

Interdimensional

I see you.

You are my mirror, clear as day.

We have the same face.

Made of the exact same materials.

Your eyes.

You, are, everything.

I am you.

13/11/20

Mehmet,

Thank you for absolutely everything.
I hope you know you mean the world to me. I hope you know I'm never actually far. If you ever need me, I'll be on the next flight to you.
You are my person.
You will always be my person.
To say I do not lust for you would be a lie, but you are so much more than that.
You are my friend.
You are my best friend.
You have my loyalty and you have my heart.
Such things cannot be nullified with mere physical distance.

Thank you for everything I'm so lucky to have met you.
I truly cannot wait for you to come visit me.
Please make it a priority as soon as it's safe.

I miss you already,

A.

18/11/20

I'm letting you go.

Thought you should know.

Carve

I want to take a knife and carve him out from
where he is buried in my body.

Charming Scream

That's the problem with us, why I'm hopeless when it comes to him. Even his shortcomings taste like sugar.

Before You, 21/01/19

Build and Empire of One

No, I'm a universe.
I am the oceans and storms.
Holy are my grandmothers and the women before them.
Holy as the wet earth after a storm, holy like the calf feeding from his mama.
I build and I fall.
I build and I fall.
It's so hard to stay alive, it's so hard to breath.
I am massive and divine, just like my mothers.
But why am I so scared?
Why am I so weak?
The intentions of my existence are not clear.
My spirit feels infinite yet, I am so tired.
They expect so much of you.
You are milk and you are bread.
You are a blanket and "cocaine".
The sun came out of you, of course you are a goddess.
Then why do you ache so much?
The times of rest are so welcoming but yet you hold the sun and his friends on your back and soul, even in your slumber.

Love Child

Who Loves You:

bones of poetry
spirit forged from teen lust
the purest of loves
spark of magic and despair
love child
formed of dirty poetry
poetry of abandoned children
no, not abandoned, forgotten.

and your spirit, so like your father's
love child
melancholy your companion
love child
sprung from magic

He Won't Be Found in The Snowstorm

He's not there.
The void fills my insides, but the wetness of the snow subdues my thirst temporarily.
Not unlike a desperate hangover,
that one that makes a desert of your tongue.
My feet are wet.
I wonder if I burned the boat and me inside it.
How would the snow feel then.
Would my ancestors feel it.
Would it cleanse our tribe.
Finally rid us of this realm or simply cause more karmic deapir.
What if I find him in there.
What if I play with his beard and wit while the snow falls.
Will it quench our thirst then.
Will he burn more than the fire.
Probably.
Light 13 candles.
One for each of your grandmothers.
One for each of mine.
That leaves us eight.
One for each of your solid hands
and one for each of your feet.

Your hair, your hair needs one.
We'll light one for my insides, where you'll live.
Then we'll burn.
We'll quench and we'll burn,
beneath the snowstorm.

Instructions For My Funeral

Let him know that I died.
Send the letters I never did,
they're already stamped.
Letters I knew wouldn't alter my reality, just add to my shame.
It is a tragic and confusing ting to feel shame in love.
How could the air leave the room only for one.
How could it have been all one-sided.
Send him my letters so he knows the sight of his face felt like home.
Felt like the home that rejects you and you have nowhere left to go.
Father, brother, lover, son.
I only ever felt safe in my grandma's arms and I only ever felt less alone in his presence.
Send him the letters I dedicated to his beard, to his anger, and his laughter.
Let him know I hated him.
Let him know I despised him.
His voice.
His smell.
His hands.
His fucking cat.

Let him know I don't know what any of it meant,
but that it made me burn.

The End

All I did for months was cry and miss him.

The truth is, that if I saw you in public, I would try to hide.
I wouldn't know how to act.

You broke my heart.

Request

I ask that you wither away any resemblance of love or care in my heart I still hold for this cynic and fool. Wither away completely Mehmet from my DNA.

So let it be. So it is.

Goodbye My Love

Life is poetry baby,

thank you for being a favourite chapter.

seni seviyorum

www.ingramcontent.com/pod-product-compliance
Lightning Source LLC
Chambersburg PA
CBHW051758130826
49812CB00033B/1192
9789357212120